I0560463

WHEN THE DOOR OPENS

Faith, Prayer, and Renewal

OMNIBUS
IN THE WILDERNESS
PRAY FOR STRONG DEMAND
FAITH IS WALKING WITH GOD
IT'S NOT OVER YET

PAUL HAN

Copyright © 2025
PAUL HAN
WHEN THE DOOR OPENS
Faith, Prayer, and Renewal
OMNIBUS
IN THE WILDERNESS
PRAY FOR STRONG DEMAND
FAITH IS WALKING WITH GOD
IT'S NOT OVER YET

All rights reserved.

No part of this publication may be reproduced, distributed, or transmitted in any form or by any means, including photocopying, recording, or other electronic or mechanical methods, without the prior written permission of the author, except in the case of brief quotations embodied in critical reviews and certain other non-commercial uses permitted by copyright law.

PAUL HAN
Divine America Media Inc.
Email: paul@divineamerica.com

Published by Divine America Media
For inquiries, speaking engagements, or distribution:
paul@divineamerica.com

Printed Worldwide
First Printing 2025
First Edition 2025

Paperback: 979-8-9930214-3-0
Hardcover: 979-8-9930214-4-7
Library of Congress Control Number: 2025920338

This is a work of fiction. Names, characters, places, and incidents either are the product of the author's imagination or are used fictitiously. Any resemblance to actual persons, living or dead, events, or locales is entirely coincidental.

The views expressed in this book are those of the author and do not necessarily reflect the views of any individual or organization.

I hope this story offers even a small comfort and encouragement to someone walking their journey of faith.

Publisher Information
Courage, Tears, and The Glory – The Immigrant Who Defied the Wind
Written by Paul Han

WHEN THE
DOOR OPENS

TABLE OF CONTENTS

ENDORSEMENT

This is not merely a book to be read—it is a book to be heard.

As Jesus once said, *"Let those who have ears to hear, listen,"* I urge you to open those ears of the heart as you read.

Read it slowly, breathing with the author as you go.

There will be moments when your heart is stirred deeply.

And in those very moments, you may hear the gentle voice of God speaking personally to you.

This is a book that cannot be further condensed.

Though small in volume, it will take time to read—because between the lines, other hidden sentences will continue to emerge.

Some of them may even be written by you, the reader.

With an open heart, read patiently, and you will discover truths that can transform suffering into blessing.

This is a book to read again and again.

As the seasons of your life change, this book will come to you wearing new colors each time.

You will hear new voices even in the sentences you once overlooked.

Above all, the words of faith that the author clung to will become a surprising gift to every reader.

I believe that through this book, God will be greatly glorified.

And I also believe that many readers will receive great blessings.

– May 3, 2025

Rev. Young Gil Kim

Founding Pastor, Thanksgiving Korean Church

AUTHOR'S NOTE

- PAUL HAN

The deepest reason I wrote this book is to offer a sincere expression of gratitude to my great-grandmother, the late Chae Eunduk, who first brought the flame of faith into our family more than 90 years ago. Born into a Confucian household, she was the first to believe in Jesus. She took her grandson to church—planting a small ember of belief that would grow into a deeply rooted tree of faith. Through her, God's grace has been passed down for five and six generations, and I thank her from the bottom of my heart.

From a young age, I had a desire to write. I read books whenever I could, studied, and sought to understand what kind of writing truly moves people. Now, in this season of my life, I feel a calling to leave a trace of my journey on this earth through writing.

After nearly 40 years—almost 50—in the United States, I have witnessed countless immigrants walking through wilderness-like seasons in life. I have seen them fall and rise again, struggling through mountains and waves, and surviving not by their own strength, but through prayer, faith, and the grace of God. Their stories remained within me and eventually took shape in the form of these novels.

One pastor's closing words in a sermon have remained in my heart even after 17 years:

"Did Joseph still need God after he became successful?"

That question is still mine today. And perhaps, it is the question of many who will read this book.

In times of success, comfort, and abundance—those may be the moments when we are most tempted to walk away from God. But through this book, and through my own life, I want to say:

Even then, I still need God.

To the Lord who leads us through our entire journey, who feeds us each day, and grants us rest—

I give thanks. Amen.

IN THE WILDERNESS

PAUL HAN

PROLOGUE

I was once standing tall—surrounded by wealth, people, honor, and applause.

But one day, in the blink of an eye, I lost everything.

People who used to smile warmly turned away without hesitation.

Those who once praised me whispered rumors behind my back.

What I had built over decades collapsed within months.

And I found myself walking alone through a wilderness I never chose.

I asked God,

"Why did You allow this?"

I begged, **"How long must I endure?"**

And I wept, **"Lord, are You even there?"**

There was no answer.

Just silence.

And the long, bitter cold of the wilderness.

But in that silence,

when I had nothing left to lean on,

when even my own thoughts turned against me,

I began to hear a voice—not loud, but certain.

"I have not abandoned you.

This wilderness is not the end,

but the beginning of your new journey."

That's when I began to write.

Not to explain. Not to impress.

But simply to testify.

That even in the wilderness,

God is there.

And that, sometimes,

grace comes after everything else has been stripped away.

CHAPTER 1

A NEW LAND, A NEW BEGINNING

On March 1, 2006, I stepped off the plane at Los Angeles International Airport with a single suitcase, $300,000 in savings, and a heart full of hope. I had left behind a stable life in Korea, a graduate degree in international trade, and two decades of work and reputation. But I was determined—no, I was convinced—that America would be the place where my real life would begin.

I settled in Irvine, a quiet and pleasant city in Southern California. Clean streets, palm trees, and blue skies greeted me each morning, and for a while, I felt like I had arrived in a promised land. With no need to work immediately, I rested for the first time in years. I walked through neighborhoods, visited libraries, and spent hours reading and dreaming. I went to church every Sunday, and though I didn't know many people, I prayed with sincerity, giving thanks for this new chapter.

The first year was smooth. I furnished my small apartment with care, paid rent six months in advance, bought a modest used car, and treated myself to good meals. I even traveled to San Diego and San Francisco, exploring the vastness of this new country. I felt safe. I felt free. I felt young again.

But as time passed, a quiet unease began to settle in.

Despite my education and experience, I found it difficult to establish a business in a new country with different systems and language. I tried reaching out to a few contacts in the Korean-American business community, but no doors opened. I explored small import-export ideas, but nothing gained traction. My savings slowly began to shrink, and for the first time, I began to feel a chill in the air.

Still, I believed that my opportunity would come. I read books on entrepreneurship. I attended networking events. I even began exploring e-commerce ideas. But it all felt like learning to walk again in a foreign world.

Then, one day, a familiar voice from Korea called me.

"Hyung, you still have money left, right?" a younger acquaintance asked. "There's a way you could double it. No taxes. Just a quick investment, and you'd be surprised at the return."

I didn't say yes. But I didn't say no either.

That's when the wilderness began.

Chapter 2

When the Wilderness Begins

I t was sometime after my second year in the United States that things began to shift.

The $300,000 I had brought from Korea had steadily dwindled. The cost of living in Irvine was higher than I had expected, and despite my efforts, no business venture had taken off. A few small trade deals fell through. The contacts I had trusted disappeared after making empty promises. I had unknowingly loaned money to someone I thought was a fellow believer—only to realize later it was a scam. The loss wasn't just financial. It was a deep wound of betrayal.

Now, I had a little under $100,000 left.

And even that felt like a fragile safety net.

I began to cut back on everything—no more eating out, no more travel. I started shopping at discount stores and cooking simple meals. I kept the air conditioning off in summer and bundled up in sweaters during winter. I became more withdrawn, unsure of whom to trust. My dreams of starting a business turned into a quiet hope of simply surviving.

I remember one particular morning.

I stood in the kitchen and opened the refrigerator.

There were only a few eggs, half a jar of kimchi, and some bottled water.

My heart sank—not just because of the food, but because of what it symbolized.

Was this how it was going to be now?

I had once been someone.

In Korea, I was respected. People sought my advice. I had titles, income, and security.

But here, I was anonymous. Invisible. A man walking through a strange land, slowly losing everything that once defined him.

And yet—

there was no crime, no accident, no dramatic downfall.

Just a slow unraveling of comfort.

A wilderness doesn't always come with thunder.

Sometimes, it comes in silence.

It was during this quiet unraveling that I began to pray differently.

Not the bold, confident prayers of the first year.

But quiet, broken ones.

"Lord, I don't understand.

But I want to trust You.

Even now... even here."

CHAPTER 3

NO MORE BUSINESS, JUST FAITH

Eventually, I made the decision to close the door on business altogether.

It wasn't sudden. I had clung to hope for as long as I could—hoping that one more idea, one more connection, one more prayer might change things. But after yet another failed deal and another month of watching my savings shrink, I realized it was time to stop. Not because I had given up on life, but because I needed to surrender this part of my life to God.

That was the hardest part.

It wasn't the financial loss that hurt the most—it was the loss of identity.

I had spent decades in Korea building my career in international trade. I was proud of my reputation. I had been someone people respected, someone who could provide and plan and lead. But now, I was letting go of all that.

One morning, I sat in silence for a long time, staring at the business files I had organized so meticulously over the past few years. I opened them one by one, reviewed every email, every contract, and every name I had written down with hope. Then I closed the folders and deleted the files.

That day, I prayed a different kind of prayer.

"Lord, from this day on, I no longer want to build my kingdom.

I want to follow Yours.

I don't know what the future holds.

But I want to walk with You."

Around that time, I started attending early morning prayer services at a local Korean church.

I had no position, no expectations, no introductions. I just sat quietly in the back, listened to the Word, and knelt down in prayer.

The pastor didn't know my name.

No one knew my past.

But I knew that God was there.

Week by week, I began to feel peace—not the peace of having all the answers, but the peace of being held.

I volunteered to help the church with small tasks—stacking chairs, folding bulletins, driving elderly members to services.

Eventually, someone asked if I'd consider serving as a lay leader. Then, after some time, they asked me to serve as an elder.

I had no business title anymore.

But I was slowly discovering a new identity—

A servant. A worshiper. A man being rebuilt in the wilderness.

CHAPTER 4

A DAY WITHOUT A SMILE

Each day began to feel the same—quiet, slow, and heavy. I would wake up before dawn, drive to church for early morning prayer, then return home. Sometimes I volunteered to help elderly church members with errands. Sometimes I took long walks in the neighborhood, just to feel the sun on my face. I smiled at neighbors, but few smiled back. I watched as families rushed to school, workers hurried off to their jobs, and couples held hands at cafes. They had purpose, movement, connection.

I had silence.

My savings had dropped below $50,000.

Still enough to survive, but just enough to remind me that I couldn't go on like this forever.

I began renting a one-bedroom apartment in a more affordable area. I cooked at home—mostly rice, kimchi, and soup. I turned off lights when not needed. I bought groceries in bulk and walked whenever I could.

There was no crisis. Just quiet erosion.

And in that erosion, came isolation.

It wasn't depression exactly. It was a strange dullness.

A tiredness that went beyond the body.

I would look at my reflection and not recognize the man in the mirror.

Sometimes I would sit for hours, staring out the window, wondering if I had made a mistake coming here.

But I didn't regret seeking God.

Even in my emptiness, I still found myself saying:

"Lord, I trust You.

Even if I have nothing else, I have You."

One day, I received a package from Korea—my wife and son had finally arrived.

They had waited patiently while I prepared everything on this end, but I could no longer delay.

We moved into the small apartment together and did our best to adjust to this new life.

My wife, Ji-hyun, started making homemade kimchi to sell.

We placed handwritten ads at Korean markets, posted online, and delivered orders by car.

It was humble, tiring, and often discouraging—but it was honest work.

And somehow, in the middle of it, a small joy returned.

Not the kind of joy that laughs loudly.

But the kind that breathes.

That survives.

That thanks God in quiet whispers, even on days when there are no smiles.

CHAPTER 5

THE TRIAL BY FIRE

Trouble never seems to come alone.

After barely adjusting to life as a family of three in a cramped apartment, another storm came—this time in the form of illness. My wife, Ji-hyun, began to suffer from severe fatigue and chronic stomach pain. At first, we thought it was just stress from the move and the kimchi business, but the pain worsened. Multiple hospital visits, tests, and medications followed.

One day, after returning from a checkup, she sat on the bed, looked at me, and said quietly,

"I don't know how much longer I can keep going like this."

It felt like my insides collapsed.

I had brought her here.

I had promised her a better life.

And now she was getting sicker, not stronger.

Medical bills started piling up. Our small business slowed down. We lost regular customers. Some com-plained about prices, others simply stopped responding. The car we used for deliveries broke down. Repairs drained what little savings we had left. My son needed supplies for school, clothes for winter, basic things— and I began to feel ashamed.

I felt like I had failed as a husband, a father, a man.

One night, I couldn't sleep. I got out of bed and sat alone in the kitchen.

I looked around—at the dim light, the half-empty rice bin, the silence of the night.

Then I broke.

I wept like a child.

I wasn't even praying—just crying.

For my wife, for my son, for myself, for all the silent suffering we had endured.

And then, from deep within me, a whisper rose:

"This is the wilderness.

But I am still here."

It wasn't an answer.

It wasn't a solution.

But it was enough to breathe again.

A few days later, I returned to early morning prayer.

I knelt longer than usual.

Not asking for miracles this time, but simply saying:

"Lord, I don't know the purpose of this fire.

But don't let me lose faith inside it."

I began to read Job again. Slowly. Carefully.

His cries felt familiar. His silence felt familiar.

But his unwavering trust—**"Though He slay me, yet will I hope in Him"**—

That became my prayer.

This was the trial by fire.

But fire, I reminded myself, could refine gold.

And maybe—just maybe—God was refining me.

CHAPTER 6

A FAINT LIGHT IN THE DARKNESS

There wasn't a specific turning point.

No miraculous phone call. No sudden blessing.

Just one day—when I realized that my heart was not as heavy as the day before.

Maybe it was because I had finally stopped struggling.

I had stopped comparing myself to who I once was, or who I thought I should be.

I simply woke up, made breakfast, and gave thanks.

That in itself was grace.

We were still poor by every standard.

Our fridge was modest. Our clothes were secondhand. Our car made strange noises.

But we had each other. We had faith. And we had survived.

Ji-hyun's health began to stabilize.

She started singing again while cooking—softly at first, then louder.

My son, Jin-woo, came home from school smiling more often.

His English improved, and he made a few friends.

One evening he said,

"Dad, I think I like it here now."

I looked at him and nodded.

But inside, I wept.

God had not changed our circumstances much.

But He had changed something in us.

The pain didn't disappear.

But it became bearable.

And strangely, even beautiful.

One Sunday, as we sat in church, the pastor shared a message on 1 Thessalonians 5:18:

"Give thanks in all circumstances, for this is God's will for you in Christ Jesus."

He paused and looked around the congregation.

Then he said, "If you're in the middle of a wilderness—give thanks. That's the door out."

Those words struck me like lightning.

Give thanks.

Not after the breakthrough,

but in the middle of the wilderness.

That afternoon, I went home and opened a blank notebook.

At the top of the page, I wrote:

"Today, I give thanks."

And under that, I listed three things:

- My wife is still with me.
- My son smiles again.
- God has never left.

I closed the notebook and smiled for the first time in a while.

Not a smile of triumph.

But a smile born of grace.

CHAPTER 7

WHEN GOD SPEAKS

It had been months—maybe years—since I first entered the wilderness.

There were days when I wondered if I had simply imagined it all:

The calling. The promise. The whisper in my spirit that told me God had a plan.

But one thing I had learned in the wilderness was this:

God is often silent—but never absent.

One morning, during early prayer, I found myself praying differently.

Not pleading.

Not complaining.

But simply saying:

"Lord, if You speak, I will listen.

If You move, I will follow.

If You remain silent, I will still wait on You."

That prayer didn't come from discipline.

It came from brokenness.

From the kind of surrender that no longer demands answers—only presence.

And then, something happened.

Not a miracle.

Not a financial breakthrough.

But a stillness—a peace I hadn't known in years.

It was like a door had quietly opened in my heart.

Not wide, but just enough to let light in.

Later that week, the pastor invited me to share a short testimony during Wednesday prayer night.

I hesitated. What could I say? That I failed? That I wandered? That I wept?

But I agreed. And when the moment came, I stood behind the podium and told the truth.

I spoke of the business that collapsed, the betrayal I experienced, the loneliness, the sickness, the fears.

And I also spoke of God's quiet faithfulness.

Of His presence in the silence.

Of the way He walked with me even when I couldn't feel it.

When I finished, the room was silent.

Then, one by one, people nodded.

Some wept. Others came to pray together.

And in that moment, I realized something profound:

Even wilderness stories can feed others.

I wasn't out of the wilderness yet.

But I was no longer lost.

Because when God speaks,

even if it's through your own broken voice,

you begin to find the way forward.

CHAPTER 8

BEYOND THE WILDERNESS

I didn't wake up one day to find that the wilderness had ended. There was no trumpet, no breakthrough email, no unexpected deposit in the bank.

But one day, I looked around and realized—I wasn't afraid anymore.

I wasn't angry, or restless, or ashamed.

Something inside me had changed.

Our life hadn't suddenly become easy.

We still lived simply.

The business never became big.

The car still made a strange sound when it rained.

But peace had moved in.

Gratitude had taken root.

And joy—not loud and boisterous, but steady and quiet—had returned to our home.

My wife and I began praying not only for our needs, but for others.

We visited elderly neighbors. We cooked for new immigrants.

We offered to pray for people in secret pain.

One afternoon, I stood on a small hill near our apartment.

The California sun was setting.

I looked back—not just at the day, but at the years behind me.

And I whispered,

"Thank You, Lord... for the wilderness."

Without it, I would never have known the depth of Your grace.

Without it, I might have stayed in the illusion of self-sufficiency.

Without it, I would not have become a man who listens, who serves, who bows.

Now, I no longer ask to leave the wilderness.

I ask only to walk with God—wherever He leads.

Sometimes, the promised land isn't a place.

It's a person.

It's the presence of God with you.

And when you find that—

you realize you've already come through.

EPILOGUE

It's been over a decade since I first entered the wilderness.

I am older now—quieter, perhaps a little slower—but also gentler, more thankful.

Looking back, I realize that the wilderness was not a detour.

It was the road I had to take.

It stripped me of everything I thought I needed—position, recognition, success.

And in the empty space that remained, God built something new.

He built trust.

He built surrender.

He built a deeper faith than I ever knew I was capable of.

There were moments I wanted to give up.

There were nights I thought I wouldn't survive.

But somehow, through prayer, Scripture, and small acts of grace, I kept walking.

And then, one day, the door opened.

Not into wealth or fame,

but into peace.

Into a life not driven by performance, but shaped by purpose.

Into a love for God that no longer depends on results, but rests in relationship.

If you are reading this and still wandering through your own wilderness—

I want to say: **don't give up.**

The door will open.

Not always how or when you expect.

But if you keep walking with God,

you'll arrive exactly where you need to be.

Because the wilderness is not the end.

It is the beginning of the life God always meant for you to live.

PRAY FOR
STRONG DEMAND

PAUL HAN

PREFACE

P rayer often feels like a last resort, but sometimes it brings deeper answers than any logic or force.

The prayer of strong demand is a persistent knocking on the door.

And this story aims to show how that door is opened.

"Pray for Strong Demand" is not merely a desperate plea to obtain something,

but a journey of transformation through a deep relationship with God—ultimately discovering love and the meaning of the life given.

This book centers on the conflicts and confessions experienced while waiting for answers to prayer and how relationships—especially within the family—are healed and transformed through that prayer.

Beyond the simple fact that prayers are answered, this story aims to show how the prayer itself opens a path to healing.

Prayer is not merely a means to get what we want,

but a powerful tool to deepen our relationship with God and to transform ourselves.

May this story bring you comfort,

and awaken the realization of how powerful prayer truly is.

Though this story is fiction, it is based on many real-life testimonies.

Prayer is not the weapon of the weak, but the greatest expression of love.

I hope that more prayers of "strong demand" arise on this earth—prayers that change lives.

CHAPTER 1

2 A.M.

The nights in Orange County are quieter than the days, and sometimes that silence feels cruel.

Han Yejin opened her eyes again. 2 a.m. She no longer needed an alarm.

She stepped out into the living room on her toes. Her husband was still asleep on the sofa with the TV on. The house was so silent, it hardly felt like the same place they had lived in for 25 years.

She sat at the kitchen table and quietly opened her worn-out Bible. Once again, Luke 11.

It was that Sunday, during Pastor Yohan's sermon, when the words of Jesus deeply touched her heart.

"It's the story of a man who goes to his friend at midnight and says, 'Lend me three loaves of bread. A guest has come to me, and I have nothing to offer.'"

"Why did the friend finally give him the bread? Because he was asked persistently. Because he was earnestly pleaded with."

Since that day, Yejin never stopped praying.

Actually, she had always prayed. But from that moment on, it was different.

She no longer prayed to receive something.

She prayed because she loved.

She prayed that her son Ian was still alive. That he would come back. That his soul would not be extinguished.

That was the heart of the man who asked for three loaves of bread.

A heart that could not let a hungry soul go unfed. A heart that chose to hold onto someone to the very end.

A mother's heart.

"God, today too, I pray that child is still breathing somewhere. Even if he pretends not to know me... Lord, please meet him."

She finished praying and quietly closed her eyes.

Then suddenly, piercing through the heavy silence, the phone rang.

Rrring...

Yejin froze.

There was no one who should be calling at this hour.

Three seconds passed before she picked up—but her heart felt like it had pounded for thirty years.

"…Hello?"

Silence.

And then—breathing.

A voice opened its mouth—familiar, yet distant.

"…Mom?"

PART 1

BREAD OF LOVE

W hen did Han Yejin's life begin to fall apart? There was no single moment she could clearly remember.

Collapse, like it often does, had seeped in slowly— until one day, it stood before her as undeniable reality.

It began with her husband Jungwoo's blank expression.

Every evening after returning from the liquor store he ran, he would eat dinner in silence and lie down on the couch without saying a word.

The TV was always on, but Jungwoo never watched it.

He just became part of the wallpaper—silent, unmoving.

His words became fewer, his prayers faded, even his breathing seemed barely there.

"Business still isn't going well?" Yejin would ask.

He'd only nod once.

"It's okay. We still have God," she'd say with a gentle smile, holding his hand.

But Jungwoo's eyes were empty.

Then one day, he said it.

"I… almost got shot today."

And he said no more.

That night, Yejin couldn't sleep.

Jungwoo lay in bed for a long time with his eyes closed, then turned his back to her and muttered,

"Sometimes I think… maybe it'd be easier if I just died."

After that, he didn't get out of bed for two days.

Her son Ian fell apart even more quietly.

It started with a message from his school—chronic unexcused absences.

Then came meetings with teachers, fights with classmates, and finally—a phone call from the police.

"Your son is currently in a juvenile shelter as a runaway."

Yejin blamed herself endlessly.

Her husband, her son—she believed all of it was because of her weakness, her lack of faith.

Each night she sat in the kitchen, sipping hot water.

She tried not to cry, but the cup would soon fill with tears.

She even thought of leaving the church.

What was the point of prayer?

She had been praying like this for ten, maybe twenty years—and nothing had changed.

But she didn't leave.

Her life may have crumbled, but her faith remained—like a lamp not yet extinguished.

It was around that time that Pastor Yohan's sermon shook her again.

"Brothers and sisters, the prayers we offer often feel rejected.

But the Lord says,

'Ask, and it will be given to you. Seek, and you will find. Knock, and the door will be opened to you…'"

After that day, Yejin began to open her Bible again.

She made up her mind—not to give up on prayer, not to give up on life.

"Prayers of strong demand are not about pestering God for what we want.

They are prayers that do not stop—because they are rooted in love."

That sentence struck Yejin's heart.

She finally understood—

Her prayer was not to make her life better.

It began because she loved.

PART 2

THE HOUSE THAT RETURNED

Prayer had begun again.

But this time, it was different.

Han Yejin no longer prayed for "solutions."

Her prayers now were acts of love—calling out names, one by one.

"God… Ian.

I don't know where he is, but please protect him today.

And Jungwoo… Please turn the light on in the dark room of his heart."

2 a.m.

When the world became quietest, she prayed.

There was no one to listen, and no one to answer right away.

Yet she sat in the same spot, at the same time, every day.

On a notebook placed next to her Bible, the same short phrases were written over and over.

"Let him be alive again today."

"Let him return again today."

"Let me love again today."

One day at Saebit Church, Deacon Park approached her gently.

"Yejin, you've been coming to early morning prayer a lot lately.

Would it be okay if I ask… What's your prayer request?"

Yejin hesitated for a long moment, then nodded.

"My son ran away. It's been two months now.

I don't even know where he is. He won't answer any calls."

Deacon Park held her hand tightly.

"God will never turn away from your prayer.

He promised that when we earnestly seek, we will find.

That's His word."

From that day on, they prayed together every Friday morning.

They wept together.

They knelt together.

They cried out together.

"God, please find Yejin's son.

Even if he's far away, Your hand can still reach him.

Let the love in this mother's heart—let this prayer—reach him."

When prayer changes, the heart changes.

When the heart changes, actions change too.

Yejin began visiting the hospital more often.

Her reason was simple:

Instead of just waiting for her prayers to be answered, she wanted to care for someone else's pain first.

One day, a boy around Ian's age was brought in, injured.

Yejin gently held his hand.

"Are you okay? I'll pray for you."

The boy—whose name she didn't even know—began to cry.

That night, Yejin cried too.

Not because she thought the boy might be her son,

but because love is a miracle that pushes beyond blood—beyond our own children—to embrace someone else.

PART 3

THE PRAYER THAT DROVE HIM OUT

The phone rang just after Yejin had finished praying that early morning.

"...Mom?"

In that moment, her entire body froze.

She could never forget that voice.

And yet, at the same time, it sounded distant—strangely unfamiliar.

"...Ian?" she replied, her voice trembling.

"Yeah... It's me.

Mom, I... I'm around San Diego.

Been working... I've been okay."

His words were broken up, like he had trouble breathing.

He sounded like he was crying.

Yejin held back her tears.

What mattered most was to keep him calm.

"It's okay, Ian.

You're alive. You called me… That alone is enough.

Thank you, really."

"Mom… I was so scared.

But lately… something weird's been happening…

Every time I fall asleep, I keep seeing you praying.

That image—your prayer—keeps coming to mind."

Yejin closed her eyes in silence.

Prayer didn't just reach through words.

Sometimes, it stirred a forgotten room in someone's memory—

maybe even unlocking the door that brought a lost child home again.

A few days later, Ian sent her the address of where he'd been staying.

Yejin quietly started the car engine.

"God... today I go to deliver those three loaves of bread.

I will embrace my son again."

PART 4

STILL WAITING

Heading south on the 405 freeway, Yejin recalled the day she had first immigrated to the United States, twenty years ago.

She was scared back then too.

She couldn't speak English, she didn't know anyone.

All she had was her husband, her one-year-old son, and the name of God.

But now—

She was a mother who prayed.

She arrived at the shared house where Ian had been staying.

The wooden door was old. The air smelled of cigarettes.

And there, standing with a gaunt face, was her son.

"…Mom."

Yejin didn't say anything.

She simply embraced him.

Her child had run away,

but her prayer had never once left home.

"…I'm sorry it took me so long," Ian whispered.

"No," she said.

"God… brought us together at just the right time."

That night, Ian finally told her—

Why he had left.

What he had feared.

How far he had fallen apart.

And Yejin simply listened.

At the end of every sentence, she said one thing:

"But I still love you."

PART 5

THE NIGHT OF ANSWER

A few days later, Ian returned home.

But that wasn't the end.

In fact, it was only the beginning.

Jungwoo still didn't speak to his son.

He just left the TV on and behaved as if Ian weren't even there.

Yejin knew she couldn't fix everything.

She also knew that prayer didn't change things *instantly*.

Still, she prayed again—this time, for her husband.

"God, please shine Your light into Jungwoo's heart.

Let him feel once more that he is loved."

Then one day, after she returned from the market,

she noticed a small note left on the kitchen counter.

"I made some soybean stew—Ian's favorite.

If it's bland, feel free to season it more.

– Jungwoo"

Yejin held the note to her chest and wept softly.

Sometimes, healing doesn't start with words.

It begins with soup.

PART 6

THE HOUSE THAT BLOOMS AGAIN

For a while, things were quiet.

No one said anything special, but the simple fact that three people were now sitting together at the dinner table—that alone filled Yejin with gratitude.

In the mornings, Jungwoo woke up first.

He brewed coffee. He packed Ian's lunch.

Sometimes, he even opened the Bible before Yejin did.

"What chapter in Proverbs was it today?" Jungwoo would ask.

Yejin would smile as she answered.

Ian listened quietly to their conversations.

In the past, the house had always been filled with the noise of the TV or long sighs.

Now, it was filled with soft readings of Scripture

and the quiet breath of prayer—like air flowing gently through their home.

A family is not a place of perfection,

but a space where healing is practiced every day.

Part 7

For Someone Else

"Yejin, would you be willing to share your testimony next Friday morning?"

Deacon Park asked gently.

Yejin hesitated.

To share her pain in front of others—it wasn't an easy thing to do.

But she prayed about it.

And God told her,

"Now is the time to speak."

That Friday, at Saebit Church's early morning service,

Yejin stood at the front.

"I prayed to God hundreds of times.

I prayed for my son to come home.

I prayed for my husband to come alive again.

But before prayer changed my life…

it changed my heart."

After the service, a young woman who had been quietly weeping in the back approached and whispered:

"I have a younger brother who ran away too…

I think I'm going to start praying now."

Yejin held the young woman's hand tightly.

Prayer is contagious.

And a prayer of strong demand—

eventually, it spreads on the wings of love.

PART 8

JUNGWOO'S CONFESSION

"Hey…"

One evening, Jungwoo finally spoke first.

"That thing I never told you about…

I think I can talk about it now."

Yejin quietly sat beside him.

"There was a robbery.

That night… the man pointed a gun at my face.

He said, 'Just one answer—

Do you want to die, or give me the money?'"

Jungwoo's hand trembled.

"And in that moment,

the only thing I could think about was Ian's face.

Not money.

Not fear.

Just Ian."

"I wanted to run away.

From everything."

Yejin reached out and gently held his shaking hand.

"But… I kept seeing you praying.

Every night…

That's what held me together."

Tears rolled down Jungwoo's cheeks.

It's rare for healing to happen through words.

But in the face of love, even confessions can't remain hidden.

PART 9

PRAYERS THAT WERE INVITED

A month later, Ian came to his parents and said, "I think...
I want to go to church."

Yejin quietly nodded.

That Sunday, the three of them sat together in a pew.

The pastor's sermon was about "The Return of the Prodigal
Son."

Ian lowered his head.

Yejin gently took his hand.

"Even when we are far away," the pastor said,

"God is never far from us."

After the service, Ian sat still for a long time.

Then, slowly, he prayed:

"God,

I'll start praying too.

Like Mom prayed for me."

And in that moment, Yejin felt something—

It was like hearing God's voice again for the first time:

"I heard your prayer."

PART 10

MIRACLES COME THIS WAY

Spring was coming.

Even the cherry tree at the edge of the yard had started to bud.

Yejin opened the curtains and let the sunlight in.

It felt like an ordinary morning, but deep in her heart, she knew—a long season of waiting had come to an end.

Ian had just landed a full-time job.

It was small, but it was a job he had interviewed for on his own.

And with his very first paycheck, he came home smiling.

"Mom, Dad... I want to buy dinner tonight with my first salary."

The three of them sat in a corner booth at a little Korean restaurant, sharing bowls of soybean stew and bulgogi.

"How long has it been since we had a meal like this together?" Yejin asked.

Jungwoo smiled softly.

"It's been a while…

But maybe that time apart made this moment all the more precious."

That night, Yejin knelt once again to pray.

"God,

Now I understand.

Prayer isn't about getting something.

It's about learning Your will."

This time, she didn't cry.

Because now,

she had learned how to pray with peace.

PART 11

IAN'S LETTER

One day, while tidying up Ian's room, Yejin found a small envelope.

It said:

"To. Mom"

Mom,

When I ran away,

to be honest… I was angry at God too.

But watching you pray every single day…

somewhere deep inside, a small flame never went out.

You reminded me of the neighbor in the Bible—

the one who knocked at midnight to borrow a loaf of bread.

Your love kept knocking on that door.

And that's what brought me back home.

I think the "bread" you asked for

was probably "forgiveness."

And "hope."

And "waiting."

One day, I want to be someone

who knocks on the door like that too—

for someone else.

Yejin folded the letter

and quietly placed it between the pages of her Bible.

Some prayers don't return right away.

But in time,

they come back—

like letters sent by God.

PART 12

THE BREAD OF THAT DAY

One Friday evening, Saebit Church held a special prayer service.

The theme that night was:

"Prayer of Strong Demand."

The pastor preached, quoting the Gospel of Luke:

"The neighbor who came to borrow bread at midnight

did so because his love was urgent.

And God does not ignore that kind of persistence."

Yejin stood at the pulpit again that evening.

But this time, she wasn't trembling.

With a calm smile and a deeper conviction than before, she said:

"I was the woman who stepped out at midnight,

asking to borrow bread.

It took time for my prayers to be answered,

but now I know—

God was always inside the house,

standing by the door."

EPILOGUE

UNTIL THE DOOR OPENS

Five years later, Ian asked a young man,

"So, how long has it been since your younger sister left home?"

The young man replied, choking back tears,

"Three years…

My parents gave up.

I'm the only one still… praying."

Ian nodded.

"That prayer… will never go to waste.

I'm living proof of that."

He gave a small smile and said,

"Don't give up.

Keep knocking—

until the door opens."

That night, Yejin opened her Bible again.

A letter slipped out.

"A prayer of strong demand

is another name for love.

And love…

always,

eventually,

comes back."

She looked out the window.

A quiet night.

But she knew—

beyond the sky of that night,

someone's prayer

was being heard.

AFTERWORD

As I close this book, I want to express my heartfelt gratitude to many people.

Through these pages, I hope we are reminded of the significance of living a life of prayer—

and that we may experience the power of prayer in our own lives.

Prayer is a sacred path through which we hear God's voice.

And in that voice, we often find the true meaning of life.

With this story, I wanted to bring hope to all those who are waiting for their own answers to prayer.

Prayer often requires patience and endurance.

But I believe—

that kind of waiting leads us to the most precious place of all.

Thank you, truly,

for reading this story.

FAITH IS WALKING
WITH GOD

PAUL HAN

Foreword

This story invites readers to reflect on what it truly means to walk in faith through the life of Eunho Noh, an immigrant who arrived in the United States with nothing but prayer.

Enduring hardship, betrayal, failure, and countless setbacks, he never let go of God's hand.

His journey reminds us that faith is not about the absence of trials, but about who walks with us through them.

May this testimony touch your heart and rekindle the spark of faith within you.

CHAPTER 1

December 1987, Gimpo International Airport, Seoul.

A biting winter wind swept through the departure gate as Eunho Noh tightly held his mother's hand. Her hands, worn and calloused from a lifetime of labor, were small but warm—warmer than anything he would feel in the months to come.

"Eunho... it's going to be cold over there. Don't skip meals. And please... pray. Always."

His mother's final words choked with emotion, like a tearful prayer sending her son into the unknown. Eunho set his suitcase down, wrapped his arms around her one last time, and whispered:

"Mom, God will be with me. I'm not going alone."

***

Los Angeles International Airport.

After 14 hours in the air, Eunho stepped onto American soil for the first time. The terminal was filled with unfamiliar sounds, strange smells, and signs he couldn't read. In worn jeans and a secondhand jacket, he clutched his faded suitcase—the only thing he brought from home.

Inside were a few packets of dried seaweed, a tub of gochujang, and a small Korean Bible. His entire fortune amounted to $200 in U.S. bills tucked in his passport.

A church deacon he'd contacted in advance picked him up and brought him to a cramped, four-person apartment in Koreatown. He would sleep in the corner of the living room on a discarded mattress. That first night, he lay awake, jet-lagged and cold, staring at the ceiling in silence.

***

His first job was at a small Korean restaurant, washing dishes.

Twelve hours a day, sometimes more. Scouring grease from pots with a steel scrubber until his fingers cracked and bled.

He knew no English except "Yes" and "Sorry," but by the second week, he'd picked up "OK, boss" and "No problem."

And yet, after every shift, he sat in the same corner of the apartment, with a cardboard box as his desk and a Bible spread open before him.

At 11 PM, while the others watched TV or slept, he prayed.

"God, thank you for bringing me here. Thank you for letting me live today.

Please walk with me tomorrow, too."

The roommates found his nightly prayers strange at first, but they soon respected his quiet consistency.

He never once complained.

***

One night, he woke up to shouting outside. Car horns, drunken rants, and even what sounded like a gunshot echoed through the street.

He pulled the thin blanket over his shoulders and stared at the dark ceiling.

"God… am I really doing the right thing? Still… I'll hold on to You."

That night, he drifted into deep sleep with a strange warmth in his heart—

as if someone were gently patting his back, whispering, "You're not alone."

CHAPTER 2

DISHWASHING AND PRAYER

At 9 a.m., the back door of the restaurant swung open, and the air was filled with the smell of oil and stir-fried kimchi.

Eunho tied on his apron and stepped up to the sink, organizing a pile of cups and plates.

His hands were still cracked and bleeding from the hot water and chemicals—but he gripped the sponge and began scrubbing without a word.

"Hey, Eunho! Get those cups out faster!"

The kitchen manager barked at him, irritation in every word.

But Eunho simply nodded, head low. "Yes, sir."

He spent the whole day washing dishes, mopping floors, and carrying boxes of napa cabbage stained with chili powder.

And while he worked, he prayed in his heart.

"God, thank You for today.

Help me remember why You brought me here."

***

After his shift ended at 11 p.m., Eunho didn't go straight to bed.

Instead, he sat in the corner of the living room, where his tattered Bible waited.

The cardboard box he used as a desk sagged under its weight, but he knelt beside it, closed his eyes, and began to pray.

"Lord... I made mistakes today. I got yelled at again. But please, shape me through this.

Use me for Your glory."

Sometimes, his prayer would melt into quiet sobs, tears dripping onto the floor.

But no matter how broken he felt, he always ended with a smile—

because even in that corner of a foreign apartment, he could still feel **God's presence**.

***

One day, he dropped a plate while rushing.

It shattered loudly, and the manager exploded.

"You're worthless! Why'd we even hire you? Get out!"

Eunho froze.

He took off his apron slowly, bowed deeply, and left through the back door.

Outside, next to the dumpster, he sat down on a crate.

It was cold.

He lowered his head and whispered, tears streaking his cheeks:

"God, if this is training… I will endure it. I will still trust You."

That night, he didn't return home.

He drove to his church and parked in the empty lot.

The building was dark, but he sat on a bench outside and opened his Bible.

Psalm 34:18 appeared under his trembling finger:

"The Lord is close to the brokenhearted and saves those who are crushed in spirit."

He closed his eyes.

His life as an immigrant was lonely and harsh—but his faith was growing stronger each day.

***

A few days later, a church elder called him.

"There's a donut shop nearby. The owner needs help with prep in the early mornings. Can you take it?"

He took the job.

From 3 a.m., he rolled dough, brewed coffee, and cleaned windows.

It paid little, but it paid enough.

In the silence before sunrise, he began every shift the same way—by whispering a prayer in the dark.

"God, I see my failures more clearly now.

Thank You for this quiet place to begin again.

Let me walk with You."

***

He didn't curse the betrayal.

He didn't complain about the setback.

He held on to one truth:

Faith is walking with God—even in silence, even in pain.

And in that quiet wilderness,

God was still watching over Eunho.

CHAPTER 3

DESPAIR AND GOD'S COMFORT

Winter in Koreatown rarely brought rain, but the sky that morning was a heavy, dull gray.

The alley behind the restaurant was muddy, and the kitchen inside was more chaotic than usual.

The manager was irritable from the moment he arrived.

Deliveries were late.

Customers kept pouring in.

Eunho was washing dishes as always when, in a rush to scoop soup into a container, he spilled boiling broth.

Another worker slipped on the wet floor and lashed out at him.

"Hey! You made me fall, idiot!"

The manager turned around, face flushed with anger.

"That's it. You're done. Today is your last day."

Eunho froze.

His hands were still wet from the sink.

He looked down, then slowly removed his apron and stepped out into the cold.

***

When he returned to the apartment, the living room was crowded.

His roommates had invited friends over, and someone had spilled soju on the rug.

There was no space left for him to lie down.

He quietly gathered his few belongings into a bag and stepped back outside.

That night, he slept in an old beat-up car parked near the church.

It had no heat, no battery, no hope—just a roof over his head.

Still, Eunho prayed.

"God… why does this keep happening?

Still, I thank You.

If this is part of the road You've prepared, I'll keep walking."

***

At dawn, he walked to the church.

It was still locked, but he sat on the cold steps and opened his Bible.

He read about Joseph—betrayed by his brothers, thrown into a pit.

About David—hunted like an animal in the wilderness.

In their pain, he saw his own reflection.

Then, an elder from the church arrived and noticed him.

"Eunho, are you okay?"

Eunho didn't answer. His throat was tight, his eyes filled with tears.

The elder sat beside him and gently said:

"You're walking through the wilderness right now.

But the wilderness has an end.

God's leading never stops."

The words sank deep into his heart like a warm light.

He turned to Psalm 119:71.

"It was good for me to be afflicted so that I might learn your decrees."

**

A few days later, thanks to the elder's introduction, Eunho found a new job at a nearby donut shop.

He worked the early shift—prepping dough, making coffee, wiping glass cases.

The pay was meager, but his spirit was lighter.

In the pre-dawn silence, he whispered the same prayer each morning.

"Lord, I am starting over.

Not for my name, but for Your purpose.

Walk with me again."

***

He didn't curse those who had wronged him.

He didn't fear the empty fridge or cold nights.

What he held onto was this:

Faith is walking with God—especially when no one else walks beside you.

***

Around that time, Eunho rented a small, run-down one-bedroom apartment, preparing for his family's arrival.

It was old and drafty, with a tiny kitchen and a folding table from a garage sale,

but to him, it looked warmer than any luxury condo.

He laid out a thin mattress, stacked some ramen and gochujang in the corner,

and every night, he prayed over that space.

"Lord, my wife and son will be here soon.

Fill this home with peace—even if it's small, even if it's poor."

***

Not long after, his wife Jihyun and young son Jinwoo arrived from Seoul.

At the airport, Eunho waited with a small bouquet.

Jihyun looked tired behind her mask, but her eyes hadn't changed.

Jinwoo, still in elementary school, looked around nervously at the foreign airport.

"Eunho… do you think we can really survive here?"

He smiled gently.

"If we walk with God, even this land can become home."

That evening, they sat around the tiny table in their new home and shared their first dinner together in America.

They held hands, bowed their heads, and prayed.

And in that small apartment, for the first time in a long time,

Eunho wasn't alone.

CHAPTER 4

SIDE DISHES AND FAITH

"Maybe… we could try selling these?"

Jihyun cautiously held out a few plastic containers.

Inside were homemade pickled cucumbers, soy-marinated perilla leaves, and a tub of well-aged kimchi.

They were humble side dishes made from leftover ingredients,

but to Eunho, they smelled like the heart of home.

He looked at them for a moment, then nodded.

"Let's try it. It's all we have, but it might be enough."

***

They packed the side dishes into their old car's trunk and drove around the apartment complexes near Koreatown.

They waited by the entrances, gently asking the Korean moms walking by,

"Would you like some homemade kimchi?

We just made it—like we would for our own family."

Most people shook their heads and kept walking.

But a few paused, then returned.

"Wait… where did you buy this kimchi?"

"This perilla leaf—it tastes like my mom's."

"I haven't had this flavor since I left Korea."

One elderly woman teared up as she ate.

"Thank you… this tastes like my childhood."

***

They barely earned $30 a day—some days, even less.

But with that money, they could add an egg to their soup.

They could pay the electric bill.

And most of all, they felt hope blooming where there had only been worry.

At night, Eunho and Jihyun sat across from each other at their small kitchen table and prayed.

"Lord, please use this side dish business for Your glory.

Let this food bring comfort to someone's table.

Let Your love be tasted in every bite."

***

They handwrote small labels for each container:

"Eunho's Homemade – Prayerfully prepared, just like home."

Word began to spread.

Through church members and neighbors, through apartment bulletin boards,

the name "Eunho's Banchan" quietly found its way into people's hearts.

One day, a local market owner called.

"Can you supply kimchi and side dishes to our store?

Your food has a story—people will come for that."

***

That night, Eunho knelt by his mattress and cried for the first time in a long while.

"God… thank You.

I couldn't have imagined this.

You've turned scraps into provision.

Tears into flavor.

Despair into hope."

His hands were still rough, his fingers cracked from dishwater and prep,

but his eyes now shone with quiet strength.

***

The side dish business slowly grew.

But every evening, he knelt in the same spot and prayed the same prayer:

"Lord, let this work be Yours.

Not for my success,

but for Your name to be lifted high."

He still drove the delivery car himself.

And after finishing his rounds, he would often sit on a church bench in the early morning light and softly sing:

"Just a closer walk with Thee, grant it, Jesus, is my plea…"

On that road—through struggle, side dishes, and prayer—

God was still walking with him.

CHAPTER 5

THE WILDERNESS TRIAL

"Mr. Noh… we've decided to launch our own brand." Eunho was speechless.

Two of his trusted employees, whom he had trained and worked with to build the side dish business, were now announcing their departure.

They weren't just quitting—they were starting a direct competitor, using what they had learned from him.

"Thanks for everything, hyung. But… we need to make a living too."

Their words were smooth, but Eunho could hear the ambition behind them—no gratitude, no humility, only calculation.

***

Within weeks, they had copied almost everything—his recipes, packaging style, even the name.

Customers were confused. Orders slowed. Revenues dropped.

At night, Jihyun wept.

"How could they… after everything we did for them?"

Eunho sat silently, then opened his Bible.

He found the story of Joseph again—sold by his brothers, imprisoned unjustly—yet never once did he curse God.

He closed the Bible and said softly:

"Let's entrust it to God.

Let's not expect reward from people.

We obeyed God with sincerity—that's enough."

***

Betrayal hurt more than poverty.

Failure felt colder than hunger.

The bank rejected their loan.

Their store contracts were canceled.

Left with unsold kimchi in the fridge, Eunho sat on the warehouse floor, defeated.

But even in that silence, he whispered,

"Lord, You're shaping me through this… right?

This isn't the end—this is a new beginning… isn't it?"

In that moment, a verse came to mind:

"The wilderness road is long, but it ends in the Promised Land."

***

That winter was the coldest of their lives.

They couldn't pay the heating bill.

Wrapped in layers of blankets, Eunho, Jihyun, and Jinwoo huddled together in their small apartment.

Jinwoo asked, "Dad, why is it so cold?"

Eunho smiled gently and replied,

"Because we're being trained by God.

And when the training ends, something amazing will come."

His words didn't deny their hardship.

But they carried a deeper truth—

a resolve born from faith.

***

One day, their church called.

"Eunho, would you be able to donate some kimchi for our missions fundraiser?"

Though he had every reason to say no,

Eunho smiled and answered,

"Thank you for asking. I'll pray and prepare."

That night, he scraped together what ingredients he had left.

He put medicated tape on his sore fingers, tied on his apron, and made 30 tubs of kimchi.

At the church bazaar, people lined up to taste it.

Someone whispered,

"Isn't this the kimchi from that old brand? It's still so good!"

***

That day, a buyer from a local grocery chain happened to visit the fundraiser.

After one bite, he handed Eunho a business card.

"Would you consider returning to retail distribution?"

And in that moment, Eunho felt it.

God was making a way—again.

***

The business began to grow once more.

But this time, Eunho was different.

He no longer chased success.

Now, his only goal was this:

to walk faithfully with God.

"The faith I found in the wilderness," he later said,

"became the strength that helped me stand again."

CHAPTER 6

A GRACE-FILLED RETURN

"M r. Noh, have you ever considered restarting your distribution business?"

The moment the grocery buyer asked the question, something stirred in Eunho's heart.

It had been months since his business collapsed, and though the pain of betrayal still lingered, this question felt different.

But Eunho hesitated.

"I'm not sure I'm ready. Last time… I made mistakes. I trusted the wrong people. I lost everything."

The buyer smiled.

"Well, from what I tasted, you've still got the most important ingredient—honesty."

***

That night, Eunho returned home and knelt on the floor.

For a long time, he said nothing.

Then, quietly, he prayed.

"Lord, can I try again?

Not with my strength. Not for success.

But with You—only with You."

As he prayed, peace washed over him like sunlight breaking through gray clouds.

God was saying: *"Now, start again. But this time, walk step by step with Me."*

***

The new beginning was small.

No employees. No warehouse.

Just Eunho and Jihyun in their cramped kitchen, rising at 4 a.m. to make kimchi.

They labeled each jar by hand, writing Scripture on the back:

"Whatever you do, work at it with all your heart, as working for the Lord." (Colossians 3:23)

This time, they weren't just making food.

They were building a ministry with their hands.

***

Word spread again.

First through Korean churches, then to American health food stores.

PAUL HAN

Customers loved the taste—but more than that, they felt something different.

"There's a warmth in your food I can't explain," someone said.

"It tastes like prayer."

Soon, a local news station reached out.

"We're doing a story on immigrants who overcame adversity.

Would you be willing to share your story?"

On camera, Eunho sat in his small kitchen and spoke plainly:

"I'm not a successful man.

I'm just someone who fell, and was lifted by grace.

All I've learned is this—**faith is walking with God, no matter how many times you fall.**"

***

Sales grew steadily.

They were able to open a small facility.

But Eunho still drove deliveries himself.

Still wore the same apron.

Still knelt beside his bed every night to pray.

***

Each morning, he whispered the same words:

"Lord, this is Your work.

Let my hands remain humble.

Let my heart remain Yours."

And through every jar of kimchi,

every handwritten label,

every delivery made with care—

God was walking with him.

CHAPTER 7

FAITH IN THE STORM

In the spring of 2020, the world came to a halt.

The streets emptied. Stores shut down. Restaurants closed. Factories stopped.

The invisible storm of COVID-19 swept across every country, every city—

and Eunho's small business was no exception.

Delivery orders were canceled.

Hospitals and schools pulled back on contracts.

Suppliers vanished. Sales dropped more than half.

"Boss... will we still get paid this month?" one employee asked hesitantly.

Eunho took a breath, looked them in the eye, and nodded slowly.

"We'll make it happen. Somehow."

That night, he and Jihyun went to their church and knelt on the cold floor.

"Lord, here we are again, in the middle of a storm.

But we choose to walk with You.

You fed Your people in the wilderness—You can feed us now."

***

A few days later, Eunho had an idea.

"If people can't go to the market, let's bring the food to them."

They created the "Eunho Homebox"—a bundle of kimchi and side dishes packaged for home delivery.

They posted it on community bulletin boards, church chat rooms, and social media.

Then, day after day, Eunho and Jihyun loaded up the car and made deliveries themselves.

It wasn't much.

But each box came with something extra—

a handwritten note:

"May this meal bring warmth to your heart.

Prepared with prayer, sent with love."

***

One customer posted a picture of the Homebox and note on Instagram.

Thousands liked and shared it.

Local media picked up the story:

"Immigrant couple shares comfort food and hope during pandemic."

Soon, a major online retailer contacted them.

"We'd like to feature your product.

It's more than food—it's a story."

***

Business picked up again.

Eunho didn't lay off a single employee.

He gathered the team and told them:

"This company doesn't belong to me.

We're stewards of God's grace.

We make food, yes—but we're called to serve."

And those weren't just words.

Eunho still delivered boxes.

Still cleaned the kitchen.

Still prayed every night.

***

That Christmas Eve, he invited the staff and their families to the factory.

They sang hymns under a small Christmas tree, ate together, and gave thanks.

"Let everything that has breath praise the Lord," Eunho read aloud.

Then, he looked at his team.

"This year was a storm.

But God walked through it with us."

Some wept quietly.

Not out of fear, but from gratitude.

Because in the storm,

they had learned what faith really meant—walking with God when everything else was out of control.

CHAPTER 8

CARRYING THE CROSS

"Dad… I don't want to go to church anymore."

Eunho's teenage son, Jinwoo, spoke the words quietly but firmly.

Since starting high school, something had changed in him.

He no longer bowed his head at family prayers.

He slept through sermons.

And one day, Jihyun found an empty bottle and troubling photos in his room.

"Eunho… I think Jinwoo is in trouble…"

That night, Eunho prayed longer than he had in months.

"Lord… I thought the wilderness was behind us.

But now my own child is drifting.

What did I do wrong?"

***

Then came the phone call.

Jinwoo had been suspended for fighting at school.

In the principal's office, Eunho listened quietly as the accusations were read.

On the drive home, there was silence.

At a red light, Eunho finally spoke.

"Jinwoo… you don't have to be perfect.

You don't have to go to church just because we do.

But I want you to know—every night, your mom and I pray for you.

We're not angry. We're just… holding on to you."

Jinwoo said nothing.

But that night, from behind his door, a faint sound emerged—

a quiet voice singing:

"Moment by moment, I'm kept in His love…"

***

Eunho realized something profound.

Children don't grow through lectures.

They grow through love—and example.

So he stopped preaching.

And lived his faith, quietly, consistently.

***

Then came another storm.

Jihyun collapsed while doing housework.

The diagnosis: early-stage breast cancer.

Eunho sat in the hospital hallway, hands trembling, heart aching.

"Lord… why this too?

Still, if this is the cross You ask us to bear…

we will carry it."

***

The surgery went well.

During recovery, Jihyun whispered through tears:

"I heard Him speak to me…

'I will never give you more than you can bear.'"

Her words became Eunho's strength.

***

Months later, Jinwoo signed up for a short-term mission trip.

When he returned, something had changed.

He prayed before meals.

He helped at church.

One night, he looked at his father and said,

"Dad… I want to live like you."

Eunho's voice cracked.

"Son… I've made so many mistakes.

But one thing I never let go of—was God's hand.

You'll walk farther than I ever did.

Just don't let go of Him."

That night, Eunho prayed:

"Lord, even in sickness, in rebellion, in pain—

You never left us.

Your mercy carried our family through it all."

***

And so, he learned:

Faith doesn't mean we avoid the cross.

It means we carry it—

knowing Jesus walks beside us.

CHAPTER 9

FOR THE GLORY OF GOD

"Mr. Noh, congratulations! Your products are now officially contracted with nationwide retailers."

Applause broke out in the small office.

Eunho accepted the final contract quietly, his hands steady, his heart humbled.

That paper wasn't just ink and numbers—it held decades of tears, trials, prayers, and grace.

But instead of celebrating, Eunho lowered his head and whispered:

"Lord, this is not my achievement.

This is Yours.

May every part of this business reflect Your glory."

***

The business expanded rapidly.

Eunho's kimchi and side dishes filled the shelves of Korean supermarkets, health food chains, even BestCo and Sammart.

TV crews came to interview him.

Magazines ran headlines like:

"The Immigrant Who Rose with Prayer"

"Faith-Fermented Kimchi"

Whenever reporters asked the secret to his success, he always gave the same answer:

"I'm not successful.

I simply fell… and God lifted me.

That's all."

***

One broadcaster asked if he had any regrets.

Eunho replied:

"Actually, I'm most afraid of this—

succeeding without God.

That's why I still wake up before dawn to pray.

This company might bear my name,

but I want only His fingerprints to remain."

His words touched thousands.

His quiet faith encouraged immigrants, pastors, workers, and seekers across the country.

***

Eunho tithed generously and gave back to churches, missions, and struggling families.

Every staff member knew:

"We don't just sell food here.

We share grace."

***

One day, a young employee asked:

"Mr. Noh… why are you still so humble?

You could retire, write a memoir, become a speaker…"

Eunho smiled and said:

"Son, nothing I have is really mine.

I was poor, betrayed, and broken.

But God gave it all back—so how can I boast?"

He paused, then added,

"I don't fear failure anymore.

I only fear **forgetting the One who walked with me.**"

***

His old, worn Bible still sat on his desk.

The pages were stained with coffee and tears.

Taped to the front cover were his life words:

"Let me live for Your glory alone."

Each morning, he would sit, open that Bible, and pray:

"Lord, use today for Your kingdom.

Let nothing in me steal the credit.

Let me remain Your servant."

***

He was later invited to share his testimony at a large revival meeting.

He hesitated at first.

But finally stood behind the podium and began:

"I came to America with nothing but faith.

I failed.

I was betrayed.

I almost gave up.

But I never let go of God.

Because I believe this:

Faith is walking with God... even when the road breaks beneath you."

The room fell silent.

Many wept.

Many bowed their heads.

But in their hearts, one seed had been planted—

the faith that walks quietly... yet never alone.

CHAPTER 10

THE FINAL PRAYER

"Dad, the church is hosting your retirement service. Everyone's coming—even Pastor Kim is preaching."

Eunho smiled gently as his youngest daughter helped him straighten his jacket.

His once-black hair had turned silver, and his hands bore the marks of a life built by faith and labor.

Today, he would step away from the business he had built—not with regret, but with deep peace.

He had passed the company on to his son, Jinwoo.

He and Jihyun had moved into a small countryside home, where they tended to a modest garden and welcomed their grandchildren on weekends.

It was a simple life—but it was more than enough.

***

The sanctuary was packed.

In the back row sat the missionary Eunho had supported for years.

In the front sat longtime employees, fellow believers, and the church elders.

Eunho stepped up to the podium and said:

"I am nothing without God.

He broke me and restored me.

He led me through valleys and deserts.

And this is what I've learned…"

He paused and looked across the congregation.

"Faith is walking with God. All the way to the end."

He bowed his head.

Tears quietly rolled down faces throughout the sanctuary.

***

After the service, his grandson Junwoo ran up to him.

"Grandpa… I want to live like you!"

Eunho knelt down and placed his hands on the boy's shoulders.

"Junwoo, being great doesn't matter.

What matters is walking with God.

You might fall. You might feel lost.

But never let go of His hand."

That night, in the quiet of his home, Eunho opened his journal and wrote:

"March 3, 2025.

I prayed again today.

Lord, let me walk with You, even now.

Let me hold Your hand until my last breath."

***

As he looked out the window at the stars above the hills,

he felt something stir within him—

a voice not of this world, saying:

"Eunho… well done, good and faithful servant."

***

His final prayer was simple.

"Thank You, Lord.

From beginning to end,

You were always with me.

Even now… and forever."

Epilogue / Afterword

This novel was inspired by a Sunday sermon of the same title delivered in May 2008 in Buena Park, California.

Although seventeen years have passed, the message still resonates with grace and truth.

This story was written in reflection of that message, drawing parallels with the life of Joseph in the Bible, as a fictional testimony of faith.

All names, characters, and places in this story are entirely fictional and were created solely for the purpose of this narrative.

May this work offer encouragement to those walking through wilderness seasons of life, and remind us all:

Faith is walking with God.

IT'S NOT OVER YET

PAUL HAN

CHAPTER 1

THE LAST NIGHT

Orange County, Southern California. Night of November 24, 2012.

Juho Lee was sitting in the living room of his younger brother's house...

The late autumn air had a chill to it, and the sound of wind outside the window pierced deeper than usual.

"Hyung, why don't you just stay the night?"

His younger brother, Joosung, spoke gently.

"You said you were going somewhere tomorrow... where to exactly?"

"Just... going out for a drive. Been sitting around too long lately. Thought I'd get some air."

Juho avoided eye contact as he answered.

It was a lie.

He had already made up his mind:

Tomorrow morning, he would quietly bring his life to an end.

His brother's family was dozing off in front of the TV, completely unaware.

Juho quietly borrowed a guest room for the night.

As he lay there, the thought that this would be his final goodbye tightened his throat.

He tossed and turned, unable to sleep.

At 5 a.m., just before the sun rose,

he silently gathered his things and stepped out.

As he softly closed the front door, he murmured under his breath:

"Goodbye… Joosung."

CHAPTER 2

DREARY SOUTHERN CALIFORNIA

The car was silent...No radio, no music. Juho gripped the steering wheel as if retracing forty years of his life.

It was late November in Southern California.

The sky was overcast, the air was dry, and fallen leaves spun through the air before landing on the roadside.

"So this is how it ends," he thought.

He had once been a successful immigrant.

After graduating from university in Korea, he had come to America with nothing but determination.

One restaurant, then two, then three...

He worked day and night, built a family, and raised two children.

His son had gone to UCLA Medical School.

His daughter to Harvard Law.

By any measure, he had achieved the American dream.

But over the last few years, the restaurant business had begun to fade.

The number of customers dwindled, lease negotiations repeatedly failed, and the last remaining location had finally closed its doors two months ago.

"They say people can't live on bread alone...

I finally understand what that means now."

He scoffed at himself, and continued driving — slowly, but with purpose — down a road that felt increasingly final.

CHAPTER 3

A SIGN, A SUBTLE PULL

B y now, the morning sun was beginning to rise...Juho was driving slowly along the I-10 freeway, heading east through the outskirts of Los Angeles.

The air was still cold, and he kept the radio off.

On either side of the road were scattered signs of recession—closed stores, empty parking lots, faded shop signs.

Here and there, he passed signs for parks or small churches.

Then, out of the corner of his eye, a modest sign came into view:

"New Hope Church – Sunday Worship 11:00 AM"

Without thinking, he pressed the brake.

"...A church?"

He asked himself,

"I'm about to end my life... what difference would attending one more service make?"

And yet, something tugged at him—soft, invisible, persistent.

As if someone—or something—was gently holding him back.

"Well... it won't hurt to stop in before I go."

With that, he turned off the freeway.

A narrow street led him to a small white church.

It was still early, but a few cars were already parked in the lot.

"What if I run into someone I know...?"

He quietly pulled out a face mask and slipped it on. Then he pulled his cap low.

Without realizing it, his body was already tensing, as if trying to protect itself.

Even now... something in him still wanted to survive.

Chapter 4

A Strange Church, A Strange Hymn

The sanctuary was warm and calm...Soft sunlight streamed in through the stained glass windows.

The choir was rehearsing gently in the background.

Juho quietly slipped into a seat in the very back corner of the room.

He lowered his head, as if trying not to be noticed by anyone.

"Does someone like me even deserve to sit here?"

he wondered.

At that moment, the choir began their song.

"Nothing but the blood of Jesus shall save my soul..."

As the first line echoed through the sanctuary,

Juho's shoulders began to tremble.

His fingers stiffened.

Something deep inside his chest cracked and collapsed.

Tears welled up—he tried to hold them back,

but it was no use.

He whispered to himself, just barely audibly:

"What have I been running toward all these years...?"

Success.

Reputation.

Raising successful children.

Keeping up appearances.

Pride.

He had sprinted through life for those things.

But now, as he sat there with empty hands and a crushed heart,

he wondered what any of it had really meant.

No one noticed his tears.

But for the first time—perhaps in his entire life—

Juho was finally facing himself. Just as he was.

CHAPTER 5

THE SERMON – IT'S NOT OVER YET

As the hymn ended, the sanctuary fell into silence...A middle-aged pastor stepped up to the pulpit.

He wore a calm smile, a clean button-up shirt, and spoke with a soft, steady voice.

Juho glanced at him and muttered inwardly:

"He looks so ordinary... Would someone like him even understand someone like me?"

The pastor took a sip of water and gently gripped the microphone.

"Dear friends," he began.

"Today's message is titled…"

He paused and looked out into the congregation with clear, unflinching eyes.

"It's Not Over Yet."

At that moment, Juho felt as if his heart had stopped.

That single sentence pierced him like a blade.

"Some of you may be sitting here this morning,

feeling like your life is already over.

Your family may have fallen apart.

Your work may be gone.

Your body and spirit may feel exhausted.

Maybe… even God feels distant."

The pastor's voice slowed, filled with compassion.

"But perhaps, that very place you believe to be your end—

that place of collapse—

is where God wants to begin.

Even when you feel utterly broken,

God has not let go of you.

In fact, He has brought you here today."

Juho bowed his head.

His hands clenched together.

"God is saying to you:

'I have not given up on you.'

What may seem like coincidence,

may actually be grace starting to bloom."

The sanctuary remained silent,but the silence was full of weight, like thunder without sound.

Inside Juho's chest,

heat and tears began to rise—

so intense, he couldn't describe them with words.

CHAPTER 6

A TEARFUL PRAYER

The service continued...The congregation stood and sang together, but Juho remained seated in silence.

His lips didn't move, but deep inside,

he began to form a prayer—

quiet, raw, and more honest than anything he had ever prayed before.

"God...

If what the pastor said is really true,

if it's really not over...

then please, pull me out of this despair."

This wasn't like the prayers of his past.

Not the kind he used to recite for success or comfort.

This was different.

It was a cry of someone laying bare his soul,

a whisper from the very edge.

"Just once…

Give me a chance to rise again.

It's okay if no one else ever knows.

Just… don't let me give up on myself."

At that moment, a hand gently tapped his shoulder.

Startled, Juho turned.

It was the senior pastor.

"It's your first time here, isn't it?"

the pastor said with a kind expression.

"You were sitting in the back and crying quite a bit…

If you're okay with it, would you like to talk for a moment?"

Juho nodded silently.

His voice didn't come out, but something inside him— something very small, yet undeniable—

had opened.

CHAPTER 7

SILENCE IN THE CAR

As he exited the church, winter sunlight poured softly over him...But inside, his heart still felt heavy with silence. He walked slowly across the parking lot,

got into his car,

closed the door,

and started the engine.

But he didn't drive.

Not right away.

He sat in the driver's seat,

hands resting on the steering wheel,

eyes unfocused,

mind blank.

"It's not over yet."

The words from the sermon echoed in his chest again and again.

"Could it really be true...?

Could it really not be over?"

He lifted his head.

On the windshield, he imagined he could still see the lyrics from the choir's hymn.

"Nothing but the blood of Jesus shall save my soul..."

In that moment,

something shifted inside him.

For the first time in a long time,

Juho felt the faintest pull of a desire—

Not to die,

but to live.

"Dying takes courage...

But maybe, so does living."

He gripped the steering wheel tighter.

"Alright...

If it's really not over,

then I'll try again."

A single tear slid down his cheek.

But it was not a tear of despair this time.

It was the beginning—

of resolution.

CHAPTER 8

DECISION – TO RISE AGAIN

Months passed. Winter gave way to spring in Southern California…Juho had kept attending church, quietly sitting in the back each Sunday, listening to the sermons, letting the words settle like seeds into dry soil.

One day, he opened his old email account and sent a message to a longtime friend—

Sungwoo Park, a college buddy who had run a men's clothing wholesale business in Dongdaemun, Seoul for over 30 years.

They hadn't spoken in a long time, lost in their own busy lives.

To Juho's surprise, the phone rang just a few days later.

"Juho, I never thought I'd hear from you again,"

Sungwoo said, his voice sounding exactly the same.

"How are you doing?"

There was a brief pause.

Juho answered slowly, honestly.

"The restaurants are all gone.

I've lost everything.

I don't have much left, and my body… it's not what it used to be.

But… I want to try living again."

Sungwoo stayed quiet for a moment, then spoke with calm confidence.

"You've never worked in clothing, but you know business.

Managing accounts, talking to customers—same principles.

I'll put together a few styles and send them over.

You've got Korean buyers all over LA.

Go give it a shot."

As the call ended, Juho felt something he hadn't felt in a long time—

a road opening before him.

A sense of movement, of heat returning to his veins.

A week later, a package arrived from Korea.

Inside were casual men's shirts and lightweight jackets for the in-between seasons.

The prices were good. The designs had a modern, American-friendly look.

He loaded them into his car and began visiting wholesalers around LA—

Koreatown, Downtown, even smaller shops in Orange County.

There were cold stares.

Some turned him away without even listening.

But then one day, a shop owner paused, holding up a shirt.

"These are pretty clean.

I'll try a few pieces. But lower the price a little, will you?"

That night, Juho sat alone in his car and smiled.

Not because of the sale,

but because—for the first time in so long—he had a **customer** again.

"Maybe I can live.

Maybe… I deserve to.

No—**I have to**."

CHAPTER 9

NEW STEPS, WORDS ON CLOTH

Juho's new life didn't move quickly, but it moved surely...Each morning, he rose early, packed a bag of clothing samples, and drove through the winding streets of Los Angeles, visiting shops in Downtown, Koreatown, and occasionally even small boutique stores in Orange County.

Most store owners said little.

Some barely looked up.

Others dismissed him outright.

But Juho kept going.

"These are directly imported from Korea,"

he'd say calmly.

"The fabric is durable, the design is simple.

They'll sell well. And I can give you a competitive price."

One afternoon, a middle-aged woman examined the clothes in silence.

She looked at the tags, then asked,

"What brand are these? I don't see any logos or labels."

Juho smiled.

"There's no official brand yet.

But I include one of these with every order."

He reached into his bag and pulled out a small white card,

then handed it to her.

The card read:

"It's Not Over Yet."

The woman stared at it for a few seconds,

then slowly nodded.

"That's exactly what I needed to hear today."

She placed an order for two boxes of merchandise.

Juho bowed deeply, his heart full.

The orders were small.

The profit margins were thin.

But in those moments—each transaction, each handshake—

he felt something returning to him:

Life.

He continued to attend church each Sunday, sitting in the same back pew.

Sometimes, he would copy lines from the pastor's sermons onto cards,

then slip them into the shirt boxes.

He no longer saw himself as

a "successful immigrant"

or a "failed businessman."

Now, he was simply

a man living by grace,

one day at a time.

CHAPTER 10

EPILOGUE - BROKEN RISE, BROKEN DREAMS

At the end of the year, Juho received a letter from his daughter in New York—a handwritten note, pressed firmly with emotion.

Dad,

Sometimes I wonder what Mom would say

if she could see you now.

I think she would be proud.

You don't have a big restaurant anymore.

You don't have a fancy store.

But I see you walking every day

with a sample bag and quiet strength,

and to me,

that's the greatest kind of faith.

It's not over yet.

I want to live that way too.

I love you.

—Your daughter

Juho sat for a long time with the letter in his hands.

Tears fell,

but they weren't from sorrow.

They were something gentler.

Something whole.

Outside the window, the winter sun was setting over Southern California.

He rose quietly,

closed the window,

turned off the lights,

and whispered like a prayer:

"Thank you, God…

for letting me live again."

He knew now—

life would never be perfect.

There would still be hard days.

Some lonely, some uncertain.

But still…

Broken rise, broken dreams.

But even broken, I rise.

Because it's not over yet.

He was living again.

ABOUT THE AUTHOR

AUTHOR BIO – PAUL HAN

Paul Han is a Korean-American author, storyteller, and media producer whose body of work spans three central genres: inspirational Christian fiction, immigrant and business dramas, and emotionally rich romance novels.

With a deep foundation in faith and a lifelong commitment to writing, Paul's stories are known for weaving personal hardship, redemption, and hope into narratives that resonate across cultures and generations. His inspirational works — including Faith Is Walking with God, Pray for Strong Demand, In the Wilderness, and It's Not Over Yet — reflect his journey of spiritual perseverance and are beloved by readers seeking comfort and strength through grace, prayer, and God's timing.

Paul also brings decades of international business leadership into his immigrant and corporate novels, such as the Courage, Tears, and The Glory – The Immigrant Who Defied the Wind. These works offer a rare and intimate look at the trials and triumphs of those who navigate foreign lands and boardrooms with dreams and scars alike.

As a multimedia creator, Paul integrates music and film into his storytelling. His internationally acclaimed romance novella Unforgettable, My Love – Ayako was released in English, Korean, and Japanese, reaching #1 in Literature & Fiction (Japanese) on Amazon. The story was accompanied by an original OST release and is part of a growing multimedia portfolio including YouTube read-alouds, theme songs, and audiobooks.

Through multilingual publishing across Amazon (eBooks, paperbacks, and audiobooks), original music distributed via DistroKid, and emotional video story-telling on YouTube, Paul Han continues to build a cross-genre, cross-media literary world that uplifts, heals, and inspires.

Whether writing about lost love, spiritual resilience, or the immigrant pursuit of dignity, Paul's stories offer a singular message:

"No matter how far you fall — it's not over yet."

www.ingramcontent.com/pod-product-compliance
Lightning Source LLC
Chambersburg PA
CBHW070332130626
46556CB00007B/2830